In

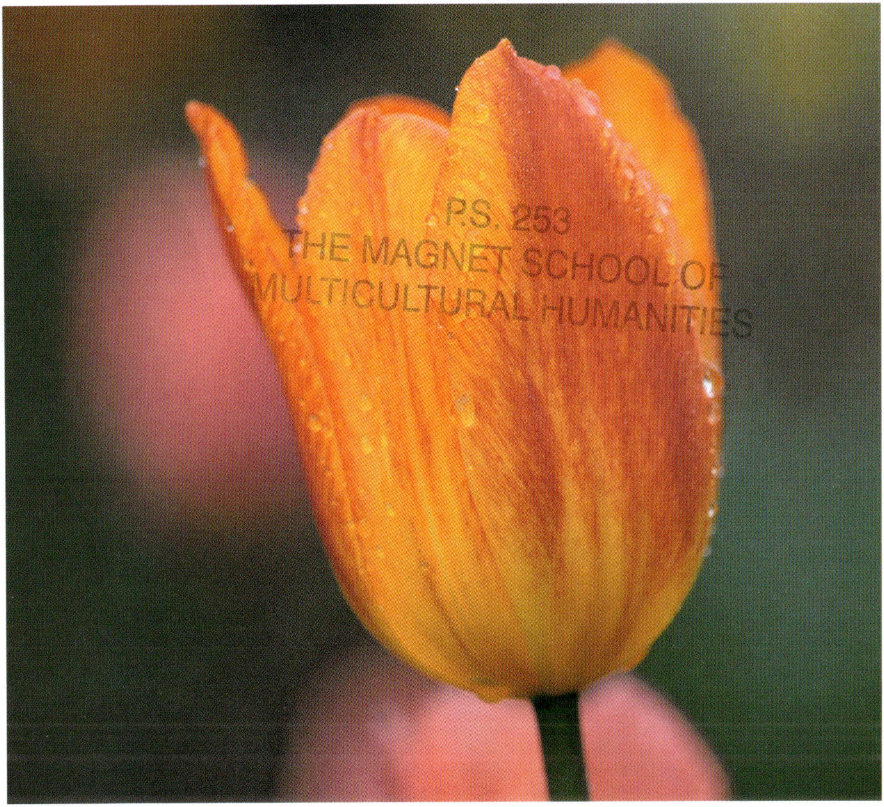

Judy Nayer

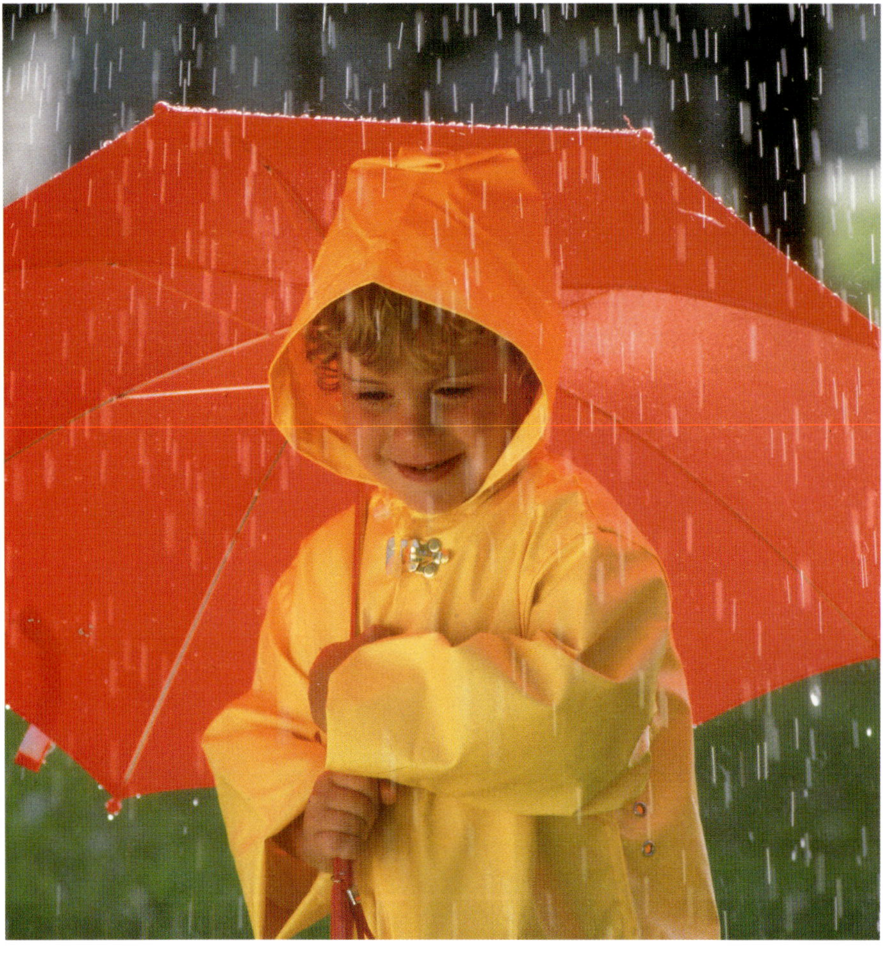

Spring rain,

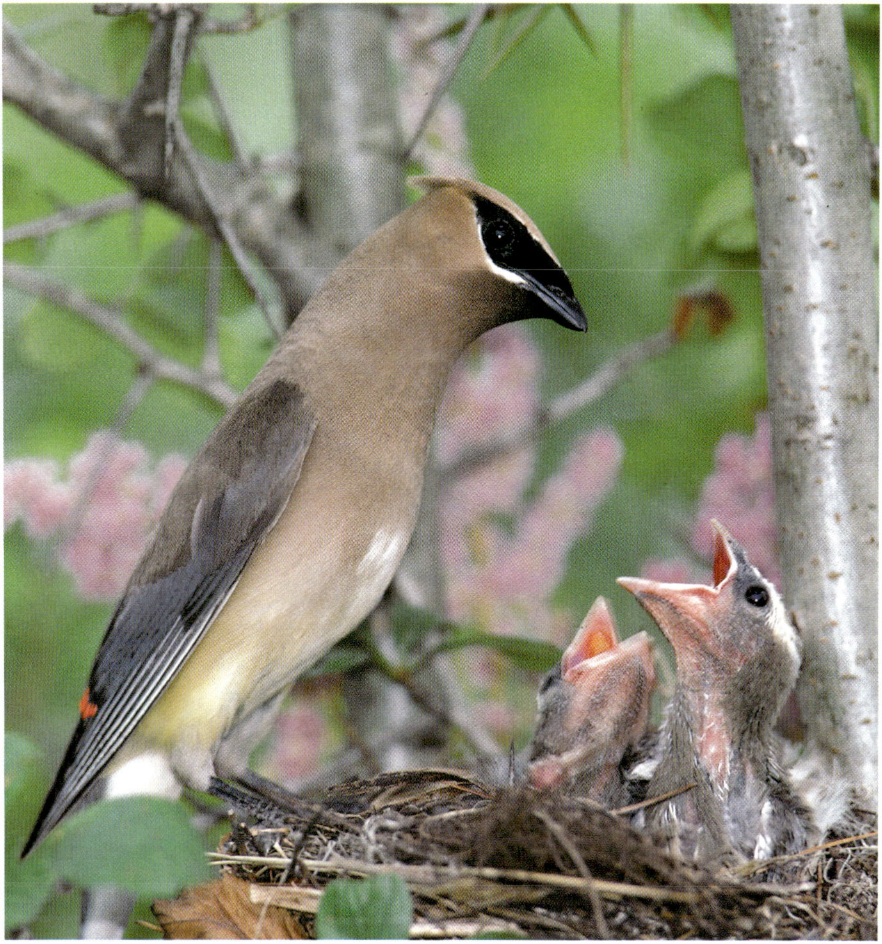

spring birds,

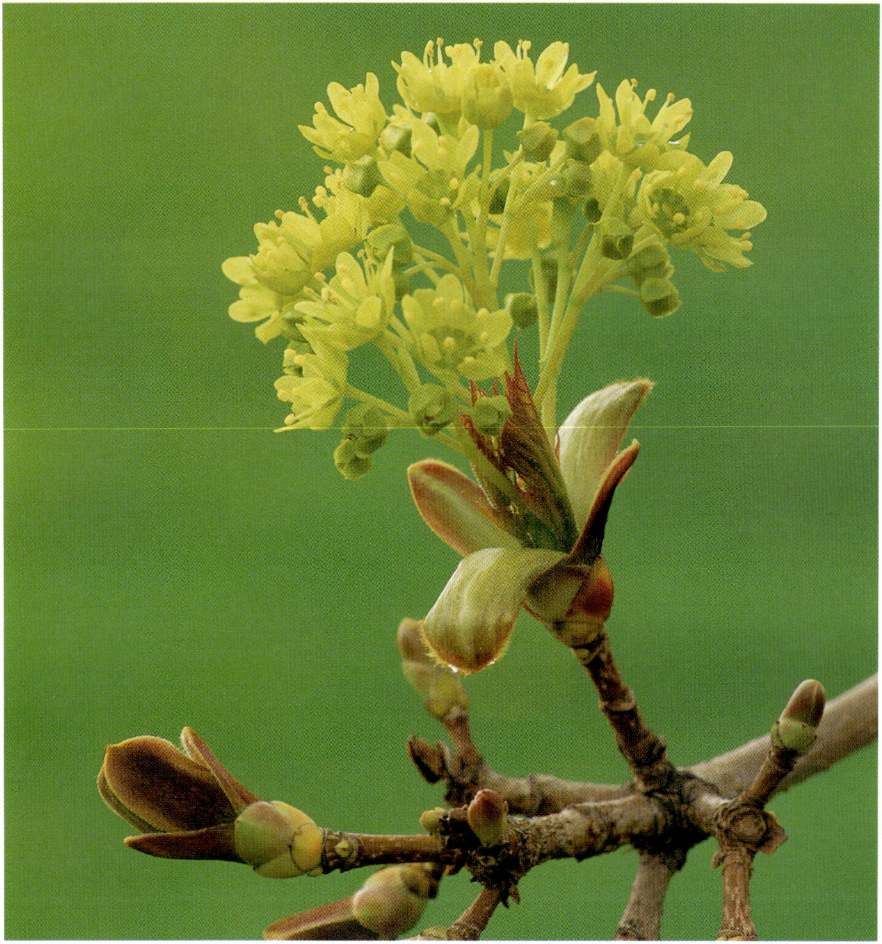

spring buds,

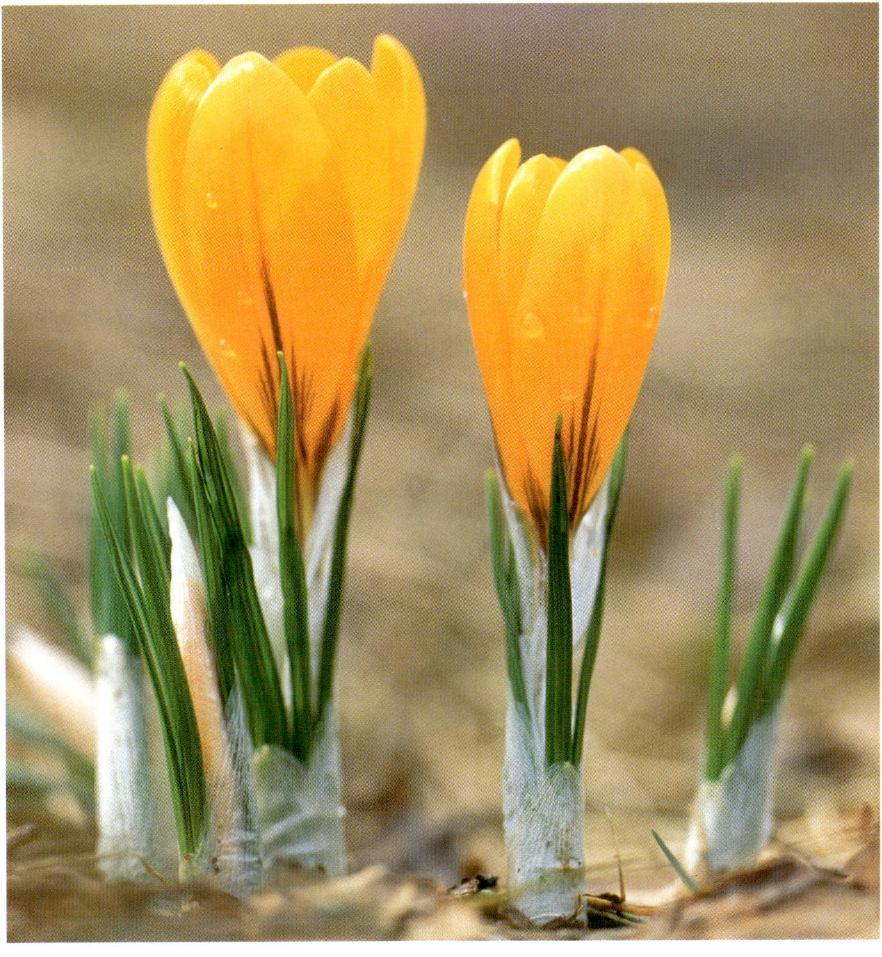

spring flowers,

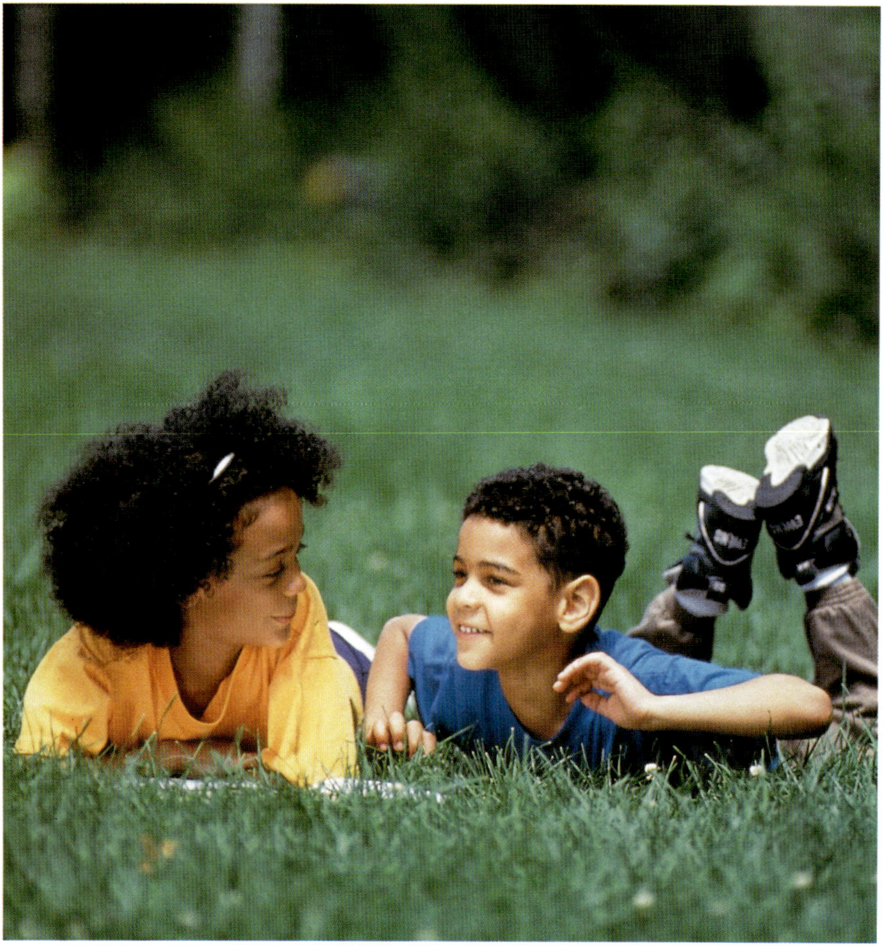

spring grass,

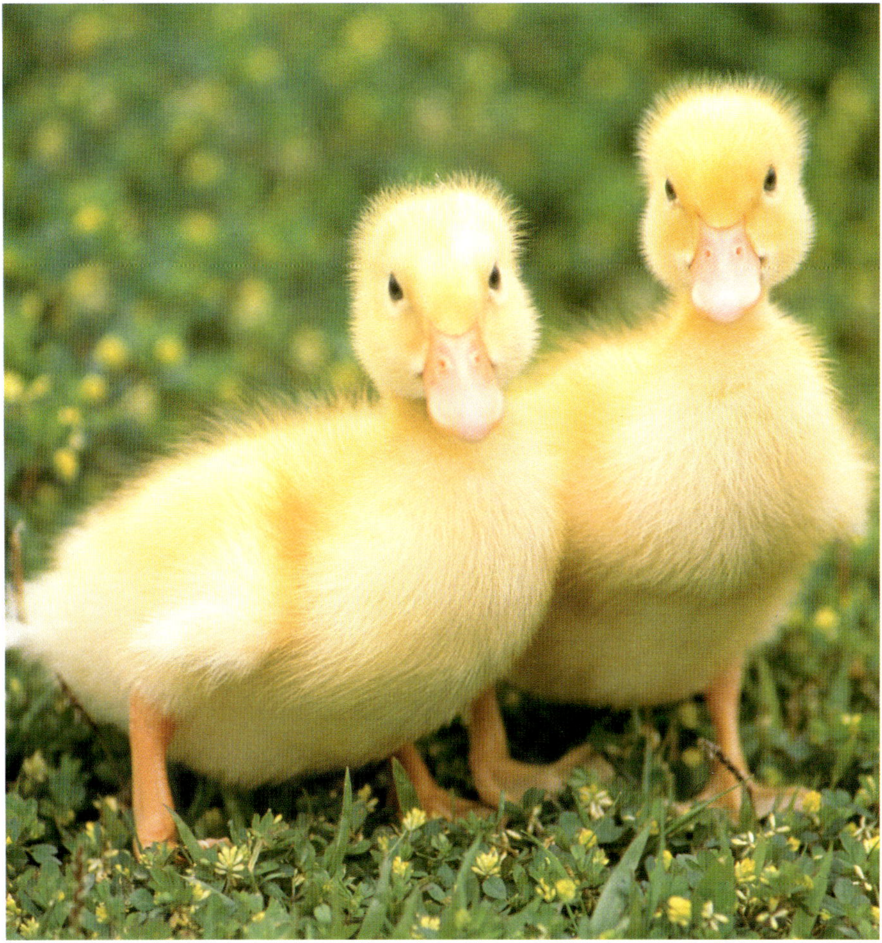

and spring ducklings.

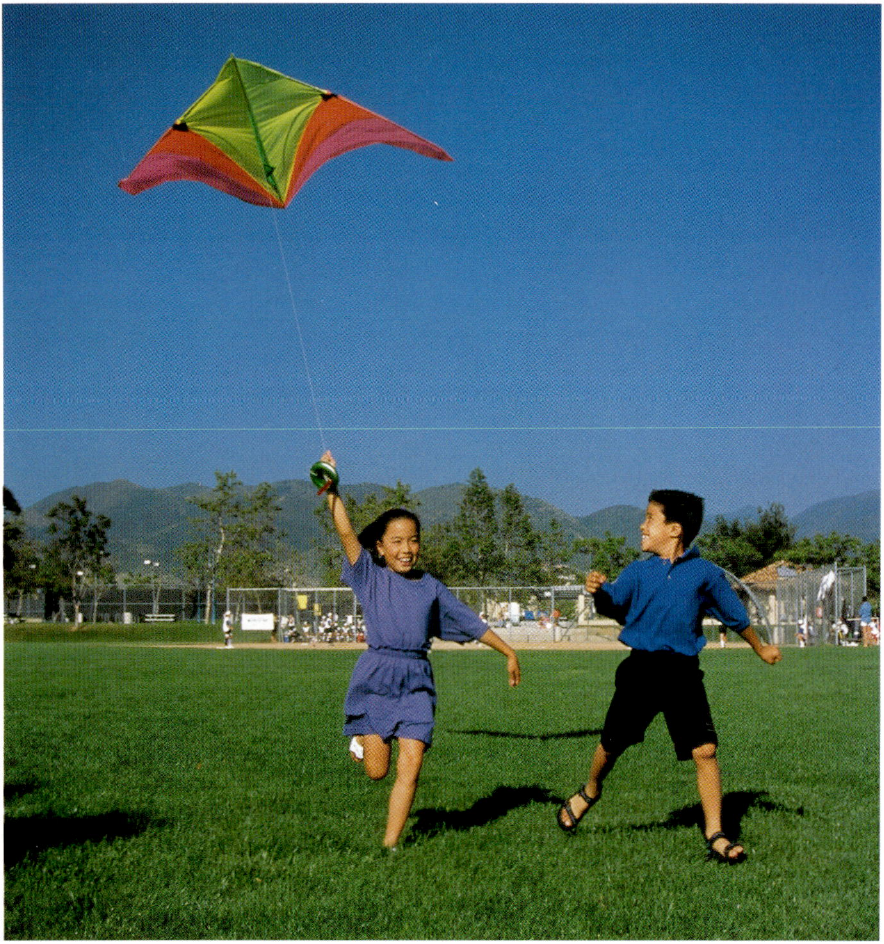

It's spring!